Bible Study
&
Meditation

Look for these topics in the Everyday Matters Bible Studies for Women

Acceptance	Mentoring
Bible Study & Meditation	Outreach
Celebration	Prayer
Community	Reconciliation
Confession	Sabbath Rest
Contemplation	Service
Faith	Silence
Fasting	Simplicity
Forgiveness	Solitude
Gratitude	Stewardship
Hospitality	Submission
Justice	Worship

Bible Study
&
Meditation

Spiritual Practices
FOR EVERYDAY LIFE

HENDRICKSON
PUBLISHERS

**Everyday Matters Bible Studies for Women—
Bible Study & Meditation**

© 2015 Hendrickson Publishers Marketing, LLC
P. O. Box 3473
Peabody, Massachusetts 01961–3473

ISBN 978-1-61970-625-5

Bible study written by Alison Gerber.

Printed in the United States of America

First Printing—June 2015

Contents

Holy Habits

Spiritual Practices for Everyday Life

Everyday life today is busier and more distracting than it has ever been before. While cell phones and texting make it easier to keep track of children and each other, they also make it harder to get away from the demands that overwhelm us. Time, it seems, is a shrinking commodity. But God, the Creator of time, has given us the keys to leading a life that may be challenging but not overwhelming. In fact, he offers us tools to do what seems impossible and come away refreshed and renewed. These tools are called spiritual practices, or spiritual disciplines.

Spiritual practices are holy habits. They are rooted in God's word, and they go back to creation itself. God has hardwired us to thrive when we obey him, even when it seems like his instructions defy our "common sense." When we engage in the holy habits that God has ordained, time takes on a new dimension. What seems impossible is actually easy; it's easy because we are tapping into God's resources.

The holy habits that we call spiritual practices are all geared to position us in a place where we can allow the Holy Spirit to work in us and through us, to grant us power and strength to do the things we can't do on our own. They take us to a place where we can become intimate with God.

While holy habits and everyday life may sound like opposites, they really aren't.

As you learn to incorporate spiritual practices into your life, you'll find that everyday life is easier. At the same time, you will draw closer to God and come to a place where you can luxuriate in his rich blessings. Here is a simple example. Elizabeth Collings hated running household errands. Picking up dry cleaning, doing the grocery shopping, and chauffeuring her kids felt like a never-ending litany of menial chores. One day she had a simple realization that changed her life. That day she began to use her "chore time" as a time of prayer and fellowship with God.

Whenever Elizabeth walked the aisle of the supermarket, she prayed for each person who would eat the item of food she selected. On her way to pick up her children, she would lay their lives out before God, asking him to be there for them even when she couldn't. Each errand became an opportunity for fellowship with God. The chore that had been so tedious became a precious part of her routine that she cherished.

The purpose of these study guides is to help you use spiritual practices to make your own life richer, fuller, and deeper. The series includes twenty-four spiritual practices that are the building blocks of Christian spiritual formation. Each practice is a holy habit that has been modeled for us in the Bible. The practices are acceptance, Bible study and meditation, celebration, community, confession, contemplation, faith, fasting, forgiveness, gratitude, hospitality, justice, mentoring, outreach, prayer, reconciliation, Sabbath rest, service, silence, simplicity, solitude, stewardship, submission, and worship.

As you move through the practices that you select, remember Christ's promise in Matthew 11:28–30:

> *Come to me, all of you who are weary and carry heavy burdens. Take my yoke upon you. Let me teach you, because I am humble and gentle at heart, and you will find rest for your souls. For my yoke is easy to bear, and the burden I give you is light.*

Introduction

to the Practice of Bible Study & Meditation

I still remember the first moment I fell in love with the Bible. I was only nine years old. A new religious education teacher had arrived at my school, and nestled in her arms lay a box full of books: twenty-five copies of the New Testament. Not the children's Bible—the real thing. She passed them out and opened her copy to Acts.

"Anyone ever read Acts before?" she asked.

No. None of us had.

"Well, let's begin."

And she did. Beginning with Acts 1:1. Week after week, line by line, this strange woman explained and brought alive to a room full of nine- and ten-year-olds the work of God after the ascension of Christ. For the first time ever we heard about tongues of fire, miraculous languages, chains breaking open, men falling out of windows, shipwrecks, island nations, and God's plan to share his good news with the entire world! It was amazing! No coloring in. No activity sheets. Just a room full of Bibles, a teacher, my classmates, and me.

I can't imagine any other book in the world gripping hold of that class, or my heart, the way the Bible did in my ninth year on Earth. Why? Because the Bible is not just any other book. It is the written word of God.

As Christians, we believe the Bible is authored by God. Theologians refer to this as the *inspiration* of Scripture, meaning that—though the books of the Bible were written by human hands and engaged their vocabularies and even personalities—the ultimate source of these words is God. "All scripture is inspired by God," says Paul in 2 Timothy 3:16.

Christians also understand the Bible to be *inerrant*, meaning that it is without error. The inerrancy of Scripture is a direct consequence of the Bible's divine authorship: that is, if God is all-powerful, it follows logically that whatever desire or design he had for Scripture, he accomplished that task with perfection. "The LORD's promises are pure," writes the psalmist in Psalm 12:6. The perfect written words of God.

But why did he write it? The answer to that question is the same for pretty much any piece of writing: so that he, the author, could communicate to us his readers.

Have you ever considered how wonderful it is that God is a talking God? He speaks—to *us*! And although he does communicate to us through a number of ways, the primary locus of his communication is, and has always been, his written word.

What did God choose to communicate through his written words? Much. In his book, we find answers to all the great questions of life: Why am I here? Is my life worth living? Why do bad things happen? Is there a God? What will happen to me after I die?

But, perhaps most remarkably, as Andrew Reid writes in *Postcard from Palestine,* the Bible "is important because it answers the questions that *God* thinks needs answering." Through it he outlines with clarity his plan for the redemption of mankind. He guides us into healthy and productive ways of living. He tells us about himself.

But if I were to open this study with a suggestion that the Bible is merely the "answer" part of a Q & A session, I would be doing the Bible a grave disservice. Because it is so much more than that. In *The Bible: A Book about Us, a Book about God,* Frederick Buechner describes the Bible as "a book about both the sublime and the unspeakable."

> *It is a book also about life the way it really is. It is a book about people who at one and the same time can be both believing and unbelieving, innocent and guilty, crusaders and crooks, full of hope and full of despair. In other words, it is a book about us.*
>
> *And it is also a book about God. If it is not about the God we believe in, then it is about the God we do not believe in. One way or another, the story we find in the Bible is our own story.*
>
> *But we find something else in it too. The great Protestant theologian Karl Barth [in* The Word of Men*] says that reading the Bible is like looking out of the window and seeing*

everybody on the street, shading their eyes with their hands and gazing up into the sky, toward something hidden from us by the roof. They are pointing up. They are speaking strange words. They are very excited. Something is happening that we can't see happening. Or something is about to happen.

Something is about to happen to you. As we work through this study together, you are about to open a window into a world of untold mysteries and challenges. A window that brings wonder to the heart of nine-year-olds and ninety-year-olds alike. A window that is a book. Not just any book. A book written by God.

CHAPTER 1

To Read Again

Returning to the Bible, Returning to God

Hilkiah the high priest said to Shaphan the
court secretary, "I have found the Book
of the Law in the LORD's Temple!"

2 KINGS 22:8

For this study, read 2 Kings 22:1–23:25.

It was that time again—that dreaded time. Home group
"share your prayer point" time.

As the question "What would you like prayer for?" circled
the room, I knew what I wanted to ask—I had wanted to ask
it for months. But I didn't ever ask it for fear of looking like
a "bad Christian," or somehow "less" than all of my other
seemingly perfect Christian friends.

I needed help getting back into the Bible.

Week after week, home group and church stirred up in me
afresh the desire to get back into God's book—to hear his

voice, to have him speak to me again, into my life. But then I'd get back home and . . . watch TV. Surf the Internet. Nap. Cook. Clean. Do *anything* but open up the Bible and read. And then, when home group rolled around for yet another session, I was faced with all the guilt and shame of having another whole week without engaging in any personal Bible study at all.

If only I knew I wasn't alone. The Center for Biblical Engagement in Lincoln, Nebraska, ran a nationwide study in 2006 to determine the Bible reading habits of devoted Christians. They found that 98.7% of those Christians surveyed believed the Bible was relevant in their everyday lives, 99.4% believed the Bible to be the inspired word of God, 96.7% believed it to be their life authority, and 94.4% believed we must read the Bible to know God. However, less than half of the survey recipients read their Bible every day.

What's wrong with us? If we know that reading the Bible is important, why don't we do it? CBE's survey found that the most common response to this question was "I don't have time." Yet, it takes the average reader only five minutes to read one chapter a day. *Five minutes!* This is about the length of time you spend *toasting bread.* Or making a cup of tea. Or patting your dog when you get home. Or setting the table for dinner. Or taking out the trash.

There are a number of different hypotheses floating around for why we *really* don't read the Bible every day. One of the more likely is that, while we know it's important, we have no *desire* to do it—or that our desire is misplaced somewhere else. Our heart—our treasure—is in the wrong place. The psalmist felt this even as he wrote, "Give me an eagerness for your laws, rather than a love for money!" (Psalm 119:36). Ask yourself: would you rather spend time in front of a mirror or spend time in front of a Gospel? Would you rather spend time at work or spend time with an Epistle? Would you rather spend time hanging out with friends or spend time hanging out with your Creator?

Here's another reason: In the twenty-first century, in the age of digital entertainment overload, we don't read the Bible because we are too distracted. We are so distracted by the unimportant that we don't devote time to the truly important. Psalm 119:37 goes on to say, "Turn my eyes from worthless things, and give me life through your word." If we carefully scrutinized our daily activity, how much time would be filled with "worthless things"? How much time is consumed by social media, online movies, DVDs, cellphone games, online shopping, real-life shopping, junk food consumption, beauty treatments, temper tantrums, and gossip? Take a good hard look at that list. Do these things really mean more to you than spending *five minutes a day* reading the Bible?

And finally, many of us find ourselves avoiding the Bible out of fear of what God might be saying in it. We know there's stuff in there about lying, coveting, jealousy, anger, unforgiveness—and we don't want to hear it. We don't want to know we're a mess. We want to hold on to our sin. In "Facing Who We Really Are" in the *Everyday Matters Bible for Women*, Kelli B. Trujillo strikes a nerve when she writes:

> *Sometimes I don't want to read the Bible. It's not because I'm lazy or tired or too busy. It's not because I've given up my faith or I doubt the Bible's inerrancy.*
>
> *It's because I know what it will say to me: it will speak truth into my life that I cannot ignore. It will point out my sins, shortcomings, and failings (2 Timothy 3:16). It will cut to the heart, exposing my 'innermost thoughts and desires' (Hebrews 4:12). It will reveal the real me—and I will not like what I see.*

Wrong priorities, wrong desires, succumbing to the distractions of our age, avoiding hearing the hard words of God—these are all the same things that led the Judeans to the place we find them in 2 Kings 22. After a succession of bad kings, the Judeans had forgotten their place as God's chosen people: rescued from slavery, fed hand-to-mouth in the desert, accompanied by his presence in a pillar of fire and smoke.

Instead, they worshipped foreign gods, seeing them as a quickstep to prosperity and political success. They engaged in detestable practices: prostitution, child sacrifice (2 Kings 21:6), and the murder of innocent people (2 Kings 21:16), to name a few. They became so encultured with the practices of their age, they were no longer distinguishable from the people God had displaced from the land before them (2 Kings 21:9).

But all of this turned around when a seeking king unearthed God's long-forgotten book, heard his words, and "turned to the LORD with all his heart and soul and strength, obeying all the laws of Moses" (2 Kings 23:25). Josiah was struck down with grief when he realized that "we have not been doing everything it says we must do" (2 Kings 22:13). He promptly sought reformation. He renewed the covenant God's people had made to serve him as their one, true God. He removed all the articles of pagan worship from their temple and countryside. He cleaned up the mess of their fallen lives. Celebration came back to their entire city. Remembrance. Thanksgiving. Worship.

Such is the power of God's book. Opening it up and reading it isn't the same as clicking on a link to a blog and reading that. The act of opening the Bible and reading those precious words all over again is, in fact, the act of picking up the receiver with God on the other end of the line. Since these are God's words, since this is the place God speaks, a return to the Bible signifies a return to him.

When I finally did get to the place where I was brave enough to ask, "Am I the only one who has difficulty reading this thing?" of course I found that I wasn't. My sister-in-law Katie was just one of the many girlfriends who resonated with my experience. She told me:

> *Just a few weeks ago, I was so desperate with life stuff, I needed something to change. I got up early in the morning, before the kids were up, before I needed to do anything, and sat out on my balcony and read the Bible.*

> *The next morning, when I opened my eyes I could see the place I'd read, just the morning before. There's a little table out there and two chairs. I looked at those chairs, and I know it sounds goofy, but I felt like one was for me and one was for God. I felt like God was saying, "I'm out here, waiting for you.*

Are you going to come sit with me today? Please?" And I did. I couldn't resist.

"The Bible is a whole series of highways, all leading towards God." —A. W. Tozer

As you study this chapter, think about how well you know the Scriptures and how often you've sought to hear and understand God's words.

1. How regularly do you read the Bible? Once a day, once a week, once a month, once a year? Make an effort to be honest now about your Bible reading regularity.

2. Without regular reading of the "Book of the Law," the Judeans lost sight of how to live for God. They had abandoned him and engaged in idol worship. What do you forget about when Bible reading is forgotten? What do you feel tempted to pursue?

3. What do you think gets in the way of your regular Bible reading? Are you too distracted, too disinterested, or too afraid? How might you overcome what stands between you and God's word?

4. Have you ever had an experience of neglecting regular Bible reading and, upon coming back to it, finding it enriching and good? Describe that experience now.

5. In an ideal world, with no time pressures or competing commitments, how often would you like to read the Bible? How much of the Bible would you like to read in one year?

6. The Center for Bible Engagement's 2006 study discovered that regular Bible readers have a few habits in common. They:

- Own a Bible;

- Keep a journal as they read the Bible;

- Use a study aid or study guide;

- Follow a reading plan;

- Read in the morning;

- Belong to a Bible study group;

- Attend Sunday school;

- Have an accountability partner; and

- Have a mentor.

Which strategy/strategies might you employ to aid you in your quest to read the Bible more regularly? Highlight them now.

"The more I studied God's Word, the more I grew to love him. And the more I grew to love him, the more I was drawn to immerse myself in Scripture." —
JoHannah Reardon, "Meeting God in Scripture"

Points to Ponder

In *A Man of One Book,* John Wesley writes:

> *I want to know one thing, the way to heaven: how to land safe on that happy shore. God himself has condescended to teach the way. . . . He hath written it down in a book. O give me that book! At any price give me the Book of God! I have it: here is knowledge enough for me. Let me be* homo unius libri *(a man of one book). Here then I am, far from the busy ways of men. I sit down alone; only God is here. In his presence I open, I read his book; for this end, to find the way to heaven.*

• As we start this study, what would you like to discover in God's book?

• What burning questions do you have about life, yourself, the world, how you should live, about God? Write down those questions now.

Prayer

God, thank you for the Bible. I admit I don't read it as often as I know I should. I'm sorry for the times I have neglected to read your words. God, where there is a lack of desire for your word, ignite in me a passion for you. Where there is distraction, help me to focus on you. And where there is fear, help me to come boldly to your throne of grace. Thank you for waiting for me there, always, waiting to speak to me. I commit myself to coming back to the Bible now, because I so want to come back to you—to find you, to hear from you.

Add your prayer in your own words.

Amen.

Put It into Practice

Since the 1970s a theory has existed that if one was to do something every single day for twenty-one days, a lifelong habit would be formed. Could it work for you? Make a commitment to read one chapter of the Bible every day, without fail, for the next twenty-one days. Not sure what to read? Try reading one of the following:

- Mark and James together
- John

- Hebrews and 1 and 2 Peter
- Twenty-one of the psalms
- 1 Kings
- Judges
- Revelation

Apart from 1 Kings and Revelation (these are twenty-two chapters long), any of these will be complete after reading just one chapter every day. That's an average of only 650 words a day, shorter than the average blog post. Start right away. We all know that a habit that begins "tomorrow" or "next week" is a habit not truly begun at all.

Take-away Treasure

In "Meeting God in Scripture" (*Everyday Matters Bible for Women*), JoHannah Reardon offers another account of coming back to the Bible and finding God. Wouldn't you like her experience to be your own?

The reason these verses spoke (and still speak) so powerfully to me was because this book I was reading for the first time was painting a picture of God. Before this . . . God was a fuzzy, benevolent being that didn't bother much with humans. But the Bible revealed a specific and extremely involved God. As I read, it was truly like discovering the pearl Jesus talked about in Matthew 13:46. . . . I marveled over and over as I read it. This book was telling me who God was! No wonder I couldn't tear myself away.

CHAPTER 2

Digging Deep

An Exercise in Bible Study

Philip ran over and heard the man reading from the
prophet Isaiah. Philip asked, "Do you understand
what you are reading?"
The man replied, "How can I, unless
someone instructs me?"

ACTS 8:30-31

For this study, read Acts 8:26–40 and Philemon.

Wouldn't it be nice if everything in the Bible was self-explanatory and easy to understand? However, as the Ethiopian eunuch discovered on his way home from Jerusalem, understanding some parts of Scripture require a little extra, outside assistance.

Perhaps you can easily identify Jesus from the Ethiopian's passage: "He was led like a sheep to the slaughter." But think for a moment: *how* do you know that this "sheep" is Jesus? Is it because you've read some other part of the Bible that described Jesus as a sheep? Is it because you've heard the story of Jesus' death retold to you at Easter time? Or is it because you've studied Acts or Isaiah or both?

How would you fare on a passage for which you *don't* have a wealth of previously attained knowledge at your disposal? How do you understand a text such as, "If the dead will not be raised, what point is there in people being baptized for those who are dead?" (1 Corinthians 15:29)? Why aren't the Israelites allowed to wear clothing made of two different kinds of thread (Leviticus 19:19)? Why does Ruth uncover Boaz's feet in Ruth 3:7? And what do any of these passages have to say to us, as Christian women, today?

When faced with parts of the Bible such as these, even the most seasoned Christian can hardly deny that there are times when comprehending the Bible requires study. But why? If the Bible is God's word, his communication to us, shouldn't it be composed in such a way that everyone can understand?

To get at the answer to this question, we return to what we know about the nature of the Bible.

It's true that the Bible is God's word, and much of it is clearly expressed and easily understood. Any competent reader can enjoy reading any of the Gospels with little outside help. Any Christian can take away from 1 Corinthians 13 what we need to learn about how to love others better. We can be challenged again by Proverbs, find solace in the Psalms, be entertained by the stories of David and Noah and Samson. I could go on.

However, the difficulty we face in understanding some parts of the Bible lies in the fact that the Bible is also God's word *realized through the hands of human writers.* While God is the author of Scripture, he also chose to write it through, utilizing, or engaging with man. The author of Scripture is an eternal God, but the people who penned the Bible were human beings, writing to other human beings.

While the Bible is not flawed by human involvement, it does mean that the books of the Bible contain both eternal words *and* all the particularities of human authors: particular language, particular history, particular geography, particular humor, particular culture, even particular units of measurement—all of which are separated from us by some two thousand years of human history.

Reading the Bible, then, is the act of simultaneously hearing God's present, living, direct-to-you voice, and also looking into the communique of a distant world. Andrew Reid, in *Postcard from Palestine*, likens reading the Bible to the experience of reading someone else's postcard in the mail: "When we read the Bible we are in fact 'eavesdropping.' There is a human author communicating to a recipient other than ourselves and we are a third party."

Imagine you came home and saw a note between your housemates that read, "Katie, tell Susan I'll be at J's until our show is done. Love, Karen." Imagine that you are Susan. From these words, you can understand right away that Karen is not at home and won't be home until later. But to determine the exact time of her arrival, you'll need to interpret who "J" is, and also what "show" she is referring to, and what its estimated end time might be. You, Susan, are the third party, the eavesdropper on this note. Between Katie and Karen there is an assumed knowledge that requires research for Susan to completely comprehend.

In Acts 8, the Ethiopian eunuch is another eavesdropper in the conversation of Scripture. He was reading from the book of Isaiah, written some eight hundred years before his birth. He was foreign to the text's land of origin. He was reading in a language not his own. It is unlikely he grew up reading this text, and it is unlikely he knew many people who did. Is it any wonder, then, that when Philip asked, "Do you understand what you are reading?" The man replied, "How can I, unless someone instructs me?"

For the Ethiopian—or us—to understand the Bible completely, because of its nature as authored by God and written by human writers, and the fact that we are culturally and historically removed from those men, study is necessary. But to end there would be telling only one side of the story, because study of the Bible is not only "necessary" but also incredibly rewarding.

As we dig deep into Scripture, our research often yields surprising results. For example, did you know that Solomon is the most likely author of Ecclesiastes? Can you imagine the richest, most successful king of Israel writing, "I observed everything going on under the sun, and really, it is all meaningless—like chasing the wind"? What an impact this makes on our understanding of the futility of chasing wealth and power. And did you know that when Jesus cried out on the cross "My God, my God, why have you abandoned me?" he was quoting a well-known psalm (Psalm 22)? This psalm describes Jesus' suffering in detail, but it also shows that God has not abandoned him—he has indeed heard him. Yet it ministers to us as well, giving us comfort in the darkest moments of our lives. What a difference that makes to Christ's words, flipping our perception of them upside down, from an attitude of abandonment and despair to one of assurance and hope.

As I was preparing to write these words, I did a little investigative Bible study of my own. I was surprised to discover that at the time Philip met the eunuch on the road to Gaza, historians find no evidence of prejudice against any race because of their color or appearance. In fact, the prevailing attitude towards the Ethiopian people was one of wonderment: ancient Greeks were amazed and intrigued by the Ethiopian appearance and culture because they were so markedly different from their own. To the Greek, Ethiopia was so different it was "quite frequently identified with the ends of the Earth," writes Ben Witherington.

This information offers a clue for the reasons of the inclusion of this passage. We were told back in Acts 1:8 that the disciples would be Christ's witnesses "in Jerusalem, throughout Judea, in Samaria, and to the ends of the earth." The book of Acts is structured this way, revealing across its pages the fulfillment of this promise. And when Philip met the Ethiopian, we see for the first time how far, how very far, God intends his good news to travel.

But my studies didn't end there—I had so many more questions to ask of this passage. For instance, why was the Ethiopian man reading Isaiah in the first place? It turns out the most likely answer to this question is that he was a Gentile follower of the Israelite God. The eunuch's journey would have taken him to Jerusalem at the time of a pilgrimage festival, and on his way home he was studying the Scriptures he had adopted as his own.

We should understand, however, that it didn't matter how passionate this Ethiopian man was about Judaism; no eunuch could fully participate in the Jewish faith. A eunuch was a castrated man, charged with attending the women's quarters of oriental courts. Deuteronomy 23:1 prohibits eunuchs, by law, from ever entering any part of the temple—a crucial component of Jewish worship. Can you imagine converting to a religion, only to be told you could never enter their church?

The eunuch's status as an outsider-convert sheds light on his question to Philip, "Why can't I be baptized?" translated in the ESV as "What prevents me from being baptized?" This isn't a throwaway line, a fancy rendering of "Baptism? Why not!" Rather, it is the Ethiopian's heart question: "Can I really be part of this? Me? Or am I going to be on the outside here, too?" Philip's response says it all. The carriage is stopped immediately. The eunuch is baptized, right then and there. The doors of the church of Jesus Christ are wide open for anyone who would believe.

Isn't it amazing how a little research on just one story uncovers the beauty of the inaugurated kingdom of God and the warm welcome of our loving Savior? The Bible is an incredible book. To say "I just take it at face value" is ignoring the beauty, complexity, and depth of what sits before you. It's like saying "I won't look at that butterfly's wing under the microscope" or "I'm not interested in looking at Saturn through the telescope" when the opportunity to do so presents itself, right then and there.

We don't only study the Bible to understand a communique between two human parties, but also to see into the mind of God. Yet that mind is still unfathomably deep. "Oh, the depth of the riches of the wisdom and knowledge of God!" sings Romans 11:33. "How impossible it is for us to understand his decisions and his ways!"

This is God's book, authored by him. Explore him. Study him. Be prepared to marvel at all you find.

"The Word of God is greater than heaven and earth . . . for it forms part of the power of God and endures everlastingly. We should, therefore, diligently study God's word, and know and assuredly believe that God himself speaks unto us." —Martin Luther

> *In this study, using a six-step method, you will do some investigative Bible study of your own, on one of the shortest books of the Bible: Philemon. Read it through before you answer the following questions.*

1. The first questions to ask when faced with a text are: What kind of writing is this? What is its *literary genre*? Is the book of Philemon poetry, law, the gospel, prophecy, apocalyptic, a narrative, an Epistle, a psalm, a work of history, a fictional tale, a parable, or something else? What do you know about this kind of writing?

2. Next, we will try to determine the *structure and flow* of this text. Try to break up Philemon into little "chunks"— that is, separate units of information. Summarize each of them in one short sentence.

3. Now we'll look closely at the text—at its individual *words*. Are there any words or terms in this passage you don't understand? Look them up in a dictionary to find their meaning. When studying Acts 8, I looked at the word *Ethiopian* and what this meant in ancient Greece. What words may have changed in their meaning from the first century to today? Try looking up these words in a commentary or Bible dictionary (some suggested resources are listed in the Leader's Guide at the back of this book).

4. Next, we'll move to outside of the text, to its *people*. Who wrote Philemon? What can you find out about the author, who he was and what he did? Who was this book of the Bible originally written for? What can you find out about them? What about the people mentioned in this story? Resources you can utilize here include Philemon, other books of the Bible, the introduction to Philemon in your Bible, and commentaries.

5. Finally, we'll look at Philemon's place in *history*. What was going on around the time and place this letter was written? It looks like the author of this letter was in jail. Why? What would that have been like? He is writing about slavery. What can you find out about the nature of slavery at this point in history?

6. After gathering all of this data, it's time to *sum up* what we've learned. In one sentence, try to describe what the book of Philemon was saying to its original reader. Now, try to write in just one sentence what God might be saying through this letter to you.

"I read novels, but I also read the Bible. And study it, you know? And the more I learn, the more excited I get." —Johnny Cash

Points to Ponder

When the Ethiopian eunuch needed help understanding Isaiah, God provided Philip in a miraculous way. Think now about your own systems of support.

- How might God be offering assistance to you, right now, to help you better understand the Bible?

- Who might be able to answer your questions (your pastor or Sunday school teacher)?

- What books could you read?

- Are there any seminaries or schools nearby where you can sit in on a lecture or audit a class?

Brainstorm a list of all the resources you have at your disposal for digging deeper into God's word.

"Does anything appear dark or intricate? I lift up my heart to the Father of Lights. 'Lord, is it not thy word, If any man lack wisdom, let him ask it of God?' . . . I then search after and consider parallel passages of Scripture, comparing spiritual things with spiritual. I meditate thereon, with all the attention and earnestness of which my mind is capable. If any doubt still remain, I consult those who are experienced in the things of God. And then, yet the writings whereby being dead, they speak." —John Wesley

Prayer

God, thank you again for your word, the Bible. In it you have created something remarkable: words from you through the language of man, colored by culture, yet enriched with the depth of your wisdom and knowledge. I want to dig deep into the Bible. I want to discover the treasures you have for me there. Help me as I study. Come alongside me and support me. Teach me. I want to learn from you. I want to learn about you.

Add a prayer in your own words.

Amen.

Put It into Practice

Study a passage of Scripture in-depth this week. Choose a small section of the Bible you would like to understand better. Using the same format we employed here in this study, compile a page of information about the following of that passage:

- *Literary genre*

- *Structure*

- *Word meanings*

- *People*

- *History*

If you are working through this study in a group, bring back your findings and share them at your next meeting, enriching one another with the treasures you uncover in your text.

Take-away Treasure

As you study, remember that you are not alone. Just as the Ethiopian had Philip miraculously running alongside his chariot, we have the Holy Spirit running alongside us. Reach out to him as you need. Remember Jesus' words in John 14:26:

"When the Father sends the Advocate as my representative—that is, the Holy Spirit—he will teach you everything and will remind you of everything I have told you."

CHAPTER 3

Don't Forget

The Importance of Memorization

"You must commit yourselves wholeheartedly
to these commands that I am giving you
today. . . . Tie them to your hands and wear
them on your forehead as reminders."

DEUTERONOMY 6:6, 8

For this study, read Deuteronomy 6:4–25.

There was one requirement for a class I was taking on the
attributes of God: memorize more than thirty Bible verses
pertaining to the scriptural evidence of God's metaphysi-
cal and moral attributes. I remember looking down at the
instructions, thinking, *There is no way I am going to fit all of
that inside my brain.*

And yet somehow I did. Every word of every verse. Contrary to my misgivings, the human mind is remarkable and
has a remarkable capacity for memory when put to the test.

Rick Warren, passionate advocate for the importance of memorizing verses from the Bible, writes:

> *You may not think you have a good memory, but you remember what's important to you. You remember the phone numbers and dates that you care about. I've heard people say they can't memorize anything, but they can quote songs from the 1960s and rattle off the statistics of their favorite baseball players.*

Consider the fact that each year, as "mental athletes" from around the United States compete in the USA Memory Championship, they memorize, among other things, 117 new names and faces within fifteen minutes, 500 random numbers in five minutes, and an entire, unpublished poem in fifteen minutes. In 2006, Joshua Foer, author of *Moonwalking with Einstein*, entered the competition to see if it was possible for a "regular" person to achieve such a feat. How did Foer perform? He won.

So it's possible. Still, why should we memorize anything these days, let alone the Bible, when we can easily access it by way of apps and websites and searchable databases? Kay Marshall Strom was of this school of thinking, until a visit to a secret house church under intense persecution changed everything. In "Hiding God's Word in My Heart" (*Everyday Matters Bible for Women*), Strom writes:

> *A little grey-haired lady—the owner of the house—shuffled in and sat at the table. She pulled a folded paper from her pocket and carefully smoothed it out. Then she took out a pencil and looked at me with eager anticipation.*

"What does she want?" I asked.

"She's waiting for you to recite some chapters from the Bible. . . . Start with Romans," the translator encouraged. "We don't have any of Romans."

. . . "I don't know any chapters from Romans," I admitted.

"Oh," the translator said. "You don't have it either?"

"Well . . . yes . . . I have it," I stammered. "I have several copies in my home. I have it on my computer too. I have it, but I don't know it . . ."

Many of us are like Kay. We are surrounded by resources—Bibles, books on the Bible, teachers of the Bible, CDs that sing verses from the Bible, and websites that can search the Bible. In "A Steady Stream of Spiritual Nourishment" (*Everyday Matters for Women Bible*), LaTonya Taylor writes, "Though I have countless spiritual resources, I'd mistaken being *surrounded* by them by actually being *fed* by them." We have it all. But we certainly don't know it all.

The Bible is not just an information source to be referenced when backing up parenting decisions or writing condolences in greeting cards. This is God's book: his self-portrait, his DNA. It demands to be *known* and internalized. It is a powerful agent for change when it is hardwired into our own DNA.

Perhaps life seems too crazy, too hectic to devote a slice of the precious time-pie of our existence to something that appears as trivial as Scripture memorization. But these are exactly the moments when we need that internal connection with Scripture the most—the times when we are at risk of forgetting God's word altogether.

Take another look at Deuteronomy 6. These verses form a part of the long sermon Moses gave to God's rescued people as they stood on the border of the land God had promised to give them. Life was about to change radically for the Israelites. Up until now they had lived in relative isolation and had depended on God to feed them their daily bread (the manna in the wilderness). Now they were about to live surrounded by excessive wealth and forces competing for their spiritual devotion. They were like children being dropped from their mother's lap right into college. In the face of this Moses utters, "You must commit yourselves wholeheartedly to these commands . . . repeat them again and again" (Deuteronomy 6:6–7).

Like the Israelites, we also face ever-increasing temptations and distractions for our attention and devotion. Aren't we, in the Western world, living "in large, prosperous cities [we] did not build"? Don't we go to malls "richly stocked with goods [we] did not produce" and "draw water from cisterns [we] did not dig"? Don't our neighbors devote themselves to other gods, attractive gods—such as success, romance, things, entertainment, happiness, and family? If we think we're somehow different from the Israelites, immune to forgetfulness of God in the face of a tidal wave of distraction, we're kidding ourselves.

When the Bible is a separate object from our own minds—merely a book on a shelf—it can be left for dead. But "hidden in our hearts," as the psalmist writes in Psalm 119:11,

God's word is our treasure, able to be recalled at the time we need it most.

That time does not restrict itself to a season of prosperity either. Scripture memorization can also be exceptionally powerful in times of grief. There's a reason Jesus comforted his disciples with these words: "But when the Father sends the Advocate as my representative—that is, the Holy Spirit—he will teach you everything and will remind you of everything I have told you" (John 14:26). Christ's words, *God's* words, would bring them comfort and peace.

Again, the memorization of Scripture is key to remembering it when we need it most. The truth is that I can't remember every verse I learned from that test on the attributes of God. But I do remember one: "The eternal God is your refuge, and his everlasting arms are under you" (Deuteronomy 33:27). Less than a month after learning that verse, I found myself suddenly having to move with my family overseas. Missing my friends, my apartment, the comfort of my daily routine, I found myself also caring for family members who were ill and struggling with unemployment. Life wasn't easy. I felt I was trapped inside the emotional equivalent of a motorized carwash half the time. But through it all, that verse stayed with me, close to my heart. In the time I needed it most, that verse and the everlasting arms that held me were one and the same.

"The word of God hidden in the heart is a stubborn voice to suppress." —Billy Graham

As you study this chapter, think about any Scriptures that come to your mind when needed. How do they bring comfort to you? How do they help you?

1. Deuteronomy 6:4 is known in Jewish tradition as the Shema ("Hear"). These words are prayed morning and night by observant Jews. It is perhaps the most important Jewish prayer—their pledge of allegiance, their twice-daily commitment to serve the one true God. Are there words in the Bible that are just as precious to you? What are they?

2. In Deuteronomy 6:8, Moses encourages God's people to tie God's commandments to their hands and wear them on their foreheads. This could be taken literally or metaphorically as an encouragement to weave God's word into all that we think and do. What is there in your life that you already do or think about daily that you could connect to a Bible verse you subsequently recall daily?

3. We often think of memorization as something that happens only in our heads, but Deuteronomy 6:7 and 6:9 offer some public and communal ways the Israelites could remember God's word. What are some ways you might outwardly declare and remember verses from the Bible, or ways you might help your friends remember Bible verses that are precious to them?

4. Take a look at Deuteronomy 6:10–16. List the things that Moses is concerned will distract God's people from his word. What prevents you from spending time memorizing Scripture?

5. There is a strong emphasis in this passage on the importance of sharing God's word with the very young. If there was just one verse from the Bible you could hardwire into the brains of the next generation of Christians, what would it be? Who could you teach that verse to today?

6. Deuteronomy 6:25 reads, "For we will be counted as righteous when we obey all the commands the LORD our God has given us." What influence might the act of memorizing Scripture have on your ability to obey God's word?

"To get the full flavor of an herb, it must be pressed between the fingers. So it is the same with the Scriptures; the more familiar they become, the more they reveal their hidden treasures and yield their indescribable riches." —John Chrysostom

Points to Ponder

Think of a Bible verse you really *know*.

• Write down that verse here:

- How did you learn it?

- What impact has it had on your life?

Prayer

Father, I get so distracted in my life from focusing on you. I'm sorry. Help my mind and my attention to get refocused, back onto you and onto the words that you have given me. I don't want to only "have" your Bible, but I also want to "know" it, just as I want to know you. Help me in my quest to remember your words. And as I work to memorize Scripture, I trust you will bring back those verses in the times I need them most.

Add your prayer in your own words.

Amen.

Put It into Practice

This week, work on committing a verse or two of Scripture to memory. Not sure what to memorize? Start with something that has recently stood out for you during your daily Bible reading, or go back to an old favorite, a verse that has always been special to you. Words that have a personal significance will stick in your head so much easier than anything else. As you work on remembering your verse, employ some of these time-tested tips to memorizing the Bible:

- Break up the verse into shorter segments that you can memorize piece by piece.

- Write the verse down on a card that you can carry with you, and be sure to look at it throughout the day.

- Hang the verse up in a few prominent places in your home.

- Sit down at your desk and write it down over and over, "studying" it.

- Say it out loud at regular intervals in the day: in the shower, in the car, in front of the mirror, as you cook.

- Pray it.

- Sing it.

- Teach it to a friend.

Highlight the techniques now that you plan to use to help you.

Take-away Treasure

Memorizing the Bible might stretch you to your mental limits, but don't get hung up on perfection. Instead, strive for the prize—the union of your heart with his word. After her experience abroad, Kay Marshall Strom had this to say about her newfound passion for memorizing Scripture:

> *Sometimes when I start to recite a portion of Scripture, I stumble and make mistakes, but I've learned it doesn't matter. I'm not learning these passages for a performance. I'm memorizing them so that the Holy Spirit can call the right Scripture to mind when I need it. He cannot bring back what I never knew. But what is hidden in my heart can never be erased.*

CHAPTER 4

Your Happy Place

How to Meditate and Why

They delight in the law of the Lord,
meditating on it day and night.

PSALM 1:2

For this study, read Psalm 1.

Psalm 1, the first psalm and in many ways the prologue to all of the psalms, begins with these words, "Oh the joys of . . ." Here is the clue that in the lines that follow, the psalmist will reveal to his readers the attributes of a life overflowing with joy.

How does one find a life filled with joy? Few of us would be immune to the desire to know the answer to this question. In fact, the world is utterly obsessed with finding the answer to this question. At the time of this writing, Amazon's list for "Happiness self-help books" (and yes, they have their own special category) stands at over 1,200 titles. In 2014, Pharrell's pop single "Happy" (with the lyric "Clap your hands if you know that happiness is the truth") sold over six million copies in the United States alone. Yet all the while, depression, suicide, and self-inflicted injuries were on the rise.

If we could only find it: the fountain, not of youth, but of happiness. The psalmist's indication of its location is so countercultural, however, that it almost seems absurd. For in Psalm 1:2, the psalmist seems to be saying that the source of delight for one whose life is overflowing with joy is . . . *the Bible*? Could it really be true that those who have joy "delight in the law of the LORD"?

If we were to write off such a proposition as an anomaly, built from a singular verse found unsupported elsewhere in Scripture, we would be wrong. Throughout the psalms there are testimonies to the happiness-inducing effects of Scripture. To name just a few: Psalm 19:7 reads, "The instructions of the Lord are perfect, reviving the soul," and then in verse 8, "The commandments of the Lord are right, bringing joy to the heart." Psalm 119 repeatedly champions the joy-bringing nature of God's word: "Your instructions are my delight" (v. 77); "If your instructions hadn't sustained me with joy, I would have died in my misery" (v. 92); and "As pressure and stress bear down on me, I find joy in your commands" (v. 143).

But how can this be possible? How can the Bible be a place where one finds joy? There might be some of you who have never experienced actual joy while reading the Bible. To some, the Bible is like exercise. In my life I've known and befriended a number of gym junkies who've told me time and again, "You should work out more often—*it's fun.*" Yet, workout after workout I still hated it, still groaned every time I had to put on my running shoes and workout clothes. That went on for years, until I found a form of physical activity I really enjoyed.

To those of you who've never enjoyed reading the Bible before, here's my suggestion: Try something different; try meditation. For most of us, the word *meditation* conjures up the image of a yogi dressed in robes, sitting cross-legged, chanting, "Ohm . . ." But did you know that well before the 1990s' obsession with New Age and Eastern spiritualties, Christians were meditating? And it's about time we started claiming back that practice for ourselves.

Historically, meditation in the Christian world has been known as *lectio divina,* or sacred reading. *Lectio divina* is meditation that is focused on the Bible. Its ancient practice is comprised of four steps:

1. *Lectio* (Reading)

2. *Meditatio* (Meditation)

3. *Oratio* (Prayer)

4. *Contemplatio* (Contemplation)

I will now set about describing each of these stages, that you might be equipped to try meditation with the Bible for yourself.

1. *Lectio*

Choose a short passage and then read it *slowly.* The notion of zooming in on one thing, one *small* thing, is contrary to the natural habits of a twenty-first-century human being. The amount of information we are faced with, and process daily, is increasing at an exponential rate. John Jefferson Davis, in his book *Meditation and Communion with God,* explains that the amount of information an American consumes each day is three times as much as in 1960. To add to that, "The amount of data generated by the Internet, computers, research labs, sensors, cameras, and phones has been growing at a compound rate of 60 percent annually." Information flows into our lives like a tsunami. But here, in the ancient practice of meditating on the Bible, we are challenged to reach into a still, small pool and scoop up a mere handful of words.

As we seek to meditate on Scripture, the challenge is to read these few words at a slow pace. The pace heightens both our attention and reverence for the text. Meditative reading reads slowly, in order to listen for God's voice speaking to us through the text. You might read the passage multiple times, or read in such a way as to linger on the individual words of the text. St. Ignatius wrote that "the voice of God . . . before reaching the heart is as weak as a light breath and scarcely agitates the air." As you read, read slowly enough to make space to listen for his divine, gentle breath.

2. *Meditatio*

Meditatio is the time for our response to God's breath, heard within the words of the text. As we meditate, we ask questions of the text. What do these words mean to my life? How is God asking me to change? It is time to imagine, to visualize what you are reading. It is time to ponder. It is time to ruminate. It is time to feel.

In "Lectio Divina" (*Everyday Matters Bible for Women*), Richard J. Foster and Carmen Acevedo liken *meditatio* to "enjoying a lovingly prepared holiday meal at

Grandmother's house." It is the slow savoring of everything God has to offer for us in his word.

In *Eat This Book*, Eugene Peterson describes *meditation* as engaging with God's words in the way a dog chews on a bone. To Peterson, meditation invites "soft purrs and low growls as we taste and savor, anticipate and take in the sweet and spicy, mouthwatering and soul-energizing morsel words" of Scripture. *Meditatio* involves chewing over, perhaps for a significant period of time, all that we have read, seen, learned, felt, and heard in the Bible.

3. *Oratio*

Oratio, the third stage of meditation on Scripture, is sometimes known as the "prayer of the heart." It is the moment we cry out to God in response to what we are hearing and feel him say to us. It is giving ourselves—our struggles, desires, fears, shortcomings—over to God. It is the moment we give in to God's will.

Oratio doesn't have to be beautiful prayers made of fancy words. Its most important feature is the act of reaching out to God. *Oratio* could be a groan or a sigh. It could be, "Have mercy on me, a sinner." It could be, "Thy will be done." It could be, "I love you."

4. *Contemplatio*

Perhaps most confusingly named of all, *contemplatio* is about God's response to us. It is the gift of a strong experience of his presence. It would perhaps be better described as communion, as *contemplatio* refers to our experience of union with God. St. John of the Cross wrote, "Contemplation is nothing else but a secret, peaceful and loving infusion of God." It is the place where your meditation is headed—to gaze at God, to be intimately focused on him and experience what is a constant reality, to know that God is always intimately focused on you. St Teresa of Avila describes contemplation as "nothing else than a close sharing between friends . . . to be alone with him who we know loves us."

This intimate connection with God is actually also described in Psalm 1. In verse 6 the psalmist writes, "The LORD watches over the path of the godly." For she who is rooted in God's word, who meditates upon it, finds that she is also under the watchful eye of her Father. This sense of "watching over" is not dissimilar to the behavior of a new mother attending to her baby with affection and concern, and with a desire to be close to her little one and provide for the child's needs. The Lord's "watching over" is not an act of distant observation, but one of close interaction, close contact, and deep affection. *Contemplatio* is the act of stopping and making time, after reading the Bible, to feel that God is caring for us as his child.

It is from this place we are able to begin to unearth how reading the Bible, or more particularly meditating on the Bible, can bring about a life of joy. For joy is the natural by-product of finding ourselves intimately connected to a loving God. The rest of the world might be on a quest for happiness, but happiness should never be the end point of our journey. The real quest is to be with God and enjoy him. Joy is just the by-product of such an encounter.

It's astounding, really, when you consider that God—the One who is the most powerful, most intelligent, most skilled, most beautiful and good of the entire universe—wants, simply, to hang out with us. But he does. He's proved it time and again. He gave his son to die on the cross to close the divide *that we made,* all so that he might be near us. So make a date with him! Create a space for him to meet with you and talk to you as you meditate on his words. It is there that you will find a truly happy place.

Q: What is the chief end of man?
A: Man's chief end is to glorify God,
and to enjoy him forever."
—Westminster Shorter Catechism

> **As you study this chapter, think about the sweet encounters you have had with God in your quiet time. When was the last time this happened?**

1. Psalm 1:2 describes those who meditate on God's word as doing so "day and night." How regularly are you reading the Bible lately? How could you spread your meditation on it throughout your day?

2. Psalm 1:3 likens those rooted in Scripture to "trees planted along the riverbank, bearing fruit each season." What kind of words would you use to describe a tree planted by a river? Which of these words describes your life right now?

3. Reflect on a period of your life when you took great delight in reading God's word. What was it then that made reading the Bible fun for you?

4. Name something you enjoy doing at present. What would it take to enjoy reading the Bible as much as that?

5. Challenge yourself to list, without looking, the four stages of *lectio divina*. Which of these stages do you fear could be the most difficult for you? Which are you most excited about?

6. In the last chapter, we discussed the importance of memorizing Scripture. What do you think is the difference between memorization and meditation? How could these two practices support each other?

"Some people like to read so many [Bible] chapters every day. I would not dissuade them from the practice, but I would rather lay my soul asoak in half a dozen verses all day than rinse my hand in several chapters. Oh, to be bathed in a text of Scripture, and to let it be sucked up in your very soul, till it saturates your heart!" —Charles Haddon Spurgeon

Points to Ponder

In *Meditation and Communion with God*, Davis writes, "Because we are united to Christ in our conversion by the Holy Spirit, God is really present to us in the prayerful, meditative reading of Scripture."

- What does it mean to you that God is *really present* as you read the Bible?

- Spend some time now imagining a space where you and God meet together, regularly. What does that space look like? What kind of things do you do together in that space?

- What would it take to make that space a reality?

Prayer

God, I haven't always enjoyed reading your word, but I want to. Ignite in me a passion to spend time meditating with the Bible. Draw me to those passages you would like me to meditate on. Help me to hear your voice. Help me to pray. And above all, as I seek you, draw near to me. I want to be close to you. Thank you for wanting to be close to me.

Add your prayer in your own words.

Amen.

Put It into Practice

Spend some time this week meditating on Scripture. Choose a passage on which to meditate. If you can't think of your own, try:

- The Sheep and the Good Shepherd (John 10:1–18)

- The Vine and the Branches (John 15:1–17)

- Life in the Spirit (Romans 8:1–17)

Work through the four stages of *lectio divina*:

1. *Lectio*, reading slowly

2. *Meditatio*, thinking about those words

3. *Oratio*, praying from your heart

4. *Contemplatio*, stopping to experience God's care for you

Don't worry if you move back and forth through the different stages. Richard J. Foster and Carmen Acevedo Butcher remind us, "These elements . . . overlap and intermingle in a circular rather than linear way." After you're done, consider writing a journal entry about the impact that meditating on Scripture had on you.

Take-away Treasure

Jonathan Edwards, one of America's greatest preachers and a key figure in the Great Awakening revival of the 1730s and '40s, also unearthed great joy in his meditation on Scripture:

> *I had then, and at other times, the greatest delight in the holy Scriptures, of any book whatsoever. Oftentimes in reading it, every word seemed to touch my heart. I felt a harmony between something in my heart, and those sweet powerful words. I seemed often to see so much light, exhibited by every sentence, and such a refreshing ravishing food communicated, that I could not get along in reading. Used oftentimes to dwell long on one sentence, to see the wonders contained in it; and yet almost every sentence seemed to be full of wonders.*

CHAPTER 5

The Bible for a Change

Being Transformed by God's Word

But don't just listen to God's Word.
You must do what it says.

JAMES 1:22

For this study, read James 1:19–27.

For the five-hundredth time, the frying pan would not fit in the cupboard. As I grunted and groaned, my husband came out to see what the problem was. "I hate my life!" I responded in a huff. He then asked, "Why does cleaning the house always put you in such a foul mood?" And with that, I ran to the bedroom, slammed the door, and flopped down on the bed. Next on my to-do list was "Read the Bible," but the last thing I felt like hearing was Jesus, Paul, or John tell me what was wrong with my attitude.

And then I had an idea. Why not read Philippians? *Philippians is the "joy" book, right?* I thought to myself. *It's all "dear friends" and "I'm so thankful for you"—no hard words in there.* I felt so clever, so smug, as if I'd outsmarted God. Until I read Philippians 2:14: "Do everything without complaining and arguing."

You have *got* to be kidding me.

What I understood about the Bible that day is that we don't simply "read" the Bible to check something off a list. We don't study the Bible purely to get smart or memorize the Bible to win Bible trivia games. As Hebrew 4:12–13 says,

> For the word of God is alive and powerful. It is sharper than the sharpest two-edged sword, cutting between soul and spirit, between joint and marrow. It exposes our innermost thoughts and desires. Nothing in all creation is hidden from God. Everything is naked and exposed before his eyes, and he is the one to whom we are accountable.

The word of God is God's megaphone. It is a tool, almost like a surgical tool, that God employs in his quest to transform us.

Since the Fall, God has been in the restoration business. He is ceaselessly working at restoring the damage within us created by sin and bridging the gulf between our dirtiness and his holiness. As we saw evidenced by Jesus' healing ministry on earth, God isn't interested only in saving us from death, but also in bringing us into a healthy and rewarding experience of life. Jesus himself said, "My purpose is to give them a rich and satisfying life" (John 10:10).

God's restoration work can be seen all around us. It is visible in the Christian who has always, secretly, skimmed a little money for themselves from the household budget, and who suddenly ceases to do so. It is seen in the crass uncle who has a newfound respect for hymns and volunteering at church. It is seen in the mother who has historically reacted angrily to her children on her self-proclaimed "bad-mood Mondays," and now finally exhibits patience and kindness to the surprise of her family. These believers are being drawn further away from their disobedience and further toward God's word. All of these believers are being restored.

How does this restorative work come about? Ultimately, it is the work of God's Spirit in us, transforming us from the inside out. God's Spirit inspires within us an obedience to God's will that was never there before. And to this end, the Holy Spirit also brings to our attention, almost *highlights*, parts of God's word that we need to apply to our lives. John 16:13a says, "When the Spirit of truth comes, he will guide you into all truth."

However, even as God speaks to us through his Spirit, we're resistant to that change. James addresses this in his letter in the portion of it you've read for this chapter. Just as a friend or spouse presents defense mechanisms as we try to gently and patiently inform them of ways they might best alter their behavior, so too is God met with the same resistance when he reaches out through his word to see transformation in you.

First, we put up defenses against God's word by *not listening to it.* Even though it's not physically possible for human beings to shut their ears, I'm sure we've all experienced the frustration of someone tuning out what we are trying to tell them, especially if what we are saying is hard for them to hear. We do this with God all the time. This is why James explicitly states, "You must all be quick to listen" (James 1:19). Remember how attentive your ears were as a child, pressed to the door of your darkened bedroom, listening for Santa Claus on Christmas Eve? If we truly desire to let God's word transform our lives, we need to be listening to his word *just like that.*

Second, we resist God's word by *not accepting it.* Have you ever had a work colleague, friend, or spouse point out an area in your life in which you need to improve, but their suggestion made you feel inexplicably angry? "You need to get fit," my husband offered, as I puffed and panted up the hill to our apartment. "Well, your eyebrows need trimming!" I replied. "And why didn't you say thank you when I minded the kids today? And I hate the way you clean the stove. And you're just like your mother!" When that itty-bitty pinprick of truth hits the broken part of our lives, it's easy to retaliate with our full armory of weapons. Instead, James encourages the harder route: To be "slow to get angry," to "humbly accept the word God has planted in your hearts" (James 1:19, 21)—ears open, head down, push the anger aside and say, "You know what? You're right."

Third, we resist God's word by *not obeying it.* How can even the best advice make any difference if it's only words, spoken and heard, but we do nothing about it? My friend Louise is a vet. When I asked her what the hardest animal she has to deal with in her job was, she said, "The owners. Because it's rare they act on the information I provide. If they did, their pets would be much, much better off." You can be sure these owners listen carefully to Louise's instructions; they just don't respond to them. Change not only needs a *hearing* but also a *happening.*

This is why James goes on to write, "Don't just listen to God's word. You must do what it says" (James 1:22). How many weeks can we go into church, hear the word of God preached, and at the time think, *It's like the preacher is speaking to me! I need to do that!* Perhaps you even walk up the aisle to the altar for prayer. But then on Monday, you wake up and do the same, messed up thing all over again.

But God is patient with us! As 2 Peter 3:9 states, "He is being patient for your sake." He waits patiently through all our defense strategies. But when that moment comes, when at last we wake up and say, "Wait. Today I will do it. Today I will live those words that I heard God speak to me"—on that day "God will bless you for doing it" (James 1:25).

Depending on where you're at right now, the concept of life change may seem too hard to follow through. Or it may simply seem like too much work. Knowing God's word is going to challenge us to action may seem, at first glance, like all he's doing is placing a burden on our already exhausting schedule. But we'd be wrong.

One afternoon, after a particularly hard day of parenting, I put the kids in their room for a nap and fell down on my bed in an attempt to get a little sleep of my own. Not five minutes had passed when I heard the master bedroom door creak open and the sound of my four-year-old son's footsteps beside my bed. *Oh, great. He's up*, I thought to myself. *Perhaps if I keep my eyes closed and pretend I'm asleep . . .* And then it began: the tugging, pushing, and pulling. I was being rolled all over the place. What was he doing? Trying to *torture* me awake?

But I was utterly mistaken. Not a moment after I thought this, he stopped, having finally pried free what he was trying to get free all along—the uncomfortable lump of blanket I had so absentmindedly plopped down on top of. And with his tiny four-year-old hands and his tiny four-year-old arms, he stretched that blanket out over my body and patted me to sleep.

It's true that God's word is there to change your life. But he's not trying to torture you or inflict you, without reason, with more to do. He's doing something good for you. He's trying to bring your life comfort. Peace. Warmth. Security. Love. Wholeness. Rest. Stop resisting the work of God. Listen to his word. Accept it. Act on it. "*Let me teach you*," says Jesus, "because I am humble and gentle at heart, and you will find rest for your souls" (Matthew 11:29).

*"Regarding God's Word, let us love it and live
in it and eat it and drink it and lie down on it
and walk on it and stand on it and swear by it
and live by it and rest in it." —A. W. Tozer*

> *As you study this chapter, consider the ways God might be prompting you to be more responsive to his word, spoken to you.*

1. Have you ever sat down with a friend or family member to share some "hard words" of advice you hoped might encourage them to grow in some way? What was frustrating about how they responded to your conversation? What was helpful? How might this inform the way you respond to God's word in the future?

2. First and foremost, James invites us to be "quick to listen" (James 1:19). How do you listen to God? How do you *avoid* listening to God? How might you become more attentive to God in your life?

3. Think back to a recent time when you found it hard to be "slow to get angry" (James 1:19)? What provoked this anger? If you could go back in time, how do you wish you had responded?

4. James signifies the importance of remembering God's challenges to us when he says, "Don't forget what you heard" (James 1:25). Imagine a friend has approached you after church, telling you that during the sermon God revealed to her that she needed to complain less. How might you propose she remember what God has said to her that Sunday? How might you help her remember?

5. Reflect on a time when *you* responded to God's word—listening to it and also doing what it said. What is better about your life as a result of this obedience? Can you say, honestly, that God has blessed you as a result?

6. Second Timothy 3:16 tells us that "all scripture . . . is useful to teach us what is true and to make us realize what is wrong in our lives." What is one "true" thing God has shared with you in your Bible reading lately? What is one thing you've realized is wrong in your life?

"The Bible is alive, it speaks to me; it has feet, it runs after me; it has hands, it lays hold of me." —Martin Luther

Points to Ponder

Take some time now to reflect on what God might be challenging you to change, through his word, in your life right now. Look over the notes you have made in this study. Search through the Bible passages you have been reading lately.

- What could God be saying to you?

- How does he want you to change and grow?

Prayer

Father God, I confess I do not always respond to your word. At times, I try my best not to hear it. At others, I feel angry with you for knowing me and seeing my sin. And worst of all, there are times I feel convicted that I need to change yet do nothing about it. Lord, help this time to be different. Help me to change according to your will. I invite you to challenge me. I welcome your restorative work in my life. I want your word, your incredible word, to transform me.

Add your prayer in your own words.

Amen.

Put It into Practice

This week, be determined not to glance in the mirror, walk away, and forget what you look like (James 1:23–24). Instead, commit to acting upon whatever you have determined God is inspiring you, through his word, to change in your life. Change is hard, and you may need help. As you move into the week, consider:

- Sharing with a Christian friend what you intend to do.

- Writing down your goal and prayerfully considering what steps you need to take to get there. Write these down too.

- Keeping a "Change Journal" to keep track for yourself how you are growing.

- Finding someone to whom you can be accountable.

- Seeking out a mentor who particularly excels in the area in which you are trying to grow.

- Gathering a friend or two to pray for you and to commit to continually praying for you as there is need.

Take-away Treasure

Since we are at the end of this study, what better "take-away treasure" to leave you with than something from the treasure chest that is the magnificent, comforting, empowering, life-changing word of God:

> *What shall we say about such wonderful things as these? If God is for us, who can ever be against us? Since he did not spare even his own Son but gave him up for us all, won't he also give us everything else? (Romans 8:31–32)*

> *I am convinced that nothing can ever separate us from God's love. Neither death nor life, neither angels nor demons, neither our fears for today nor our worries about tomorrow—not even the powers of hell can separate us from God's love. No power in the sky above or in the earth below—indeed, nothing in all creation will ever be able to separate us from the love of God that is revealed in Christ Jesus our Lord. (Romans 8:38–39)*

Aren't these words incredible? They are a mere 1/5766th of the riches of God's word available to you today. Don't stop reading. Don't stop listening. God is speaking, and he has many wonderful things he wants you to hear.

Notes / Prayer Requests

Notes / Prayer Requests

_____

_____

_____

_____

_____

_____

_____

_____

_____

_____

_____

_____

_____

_____

_____

_____

_____

_____

_____

_____

Leader's Guide

Thoughts on Where to Meet

- If you have the chance, encourage each group member to host a gathering. But make sure your host knows that you don't expect fresh baked scones from scratch or white-glove-test-worthy surroundings. Set the tone for a relaxed and open atmosphere with a warm welcome wherever you can meet. The host can provide the space and the guests can provide the goodies.

- If you can't meet in homes, consider taking at least one of your meetings on the road. Can you meet at a local place where people from your community gather? A park or a coffee shop or other public space perhaps.

- If you meet in a church space, consider partnering with another local church group and take turns hosting. How can you extend your welcome outside your group?

Thoughts on Ways to Foster Welcome

- If many of your members have a hard time meeting due to circumstances, look for ways to work around it. Consider providing childcare if there are moms who have difficulty attending, or meet in an accessible space if someone who might want to join has a disability. Does a morning time work better? Could you meet as smaller groups and then get together as a larger group for an event? Be flexible and see how you can accommodate the needs of the group. Incorporate "get to know you" activities to promote sharing. Don't take yourselves too seriously and let your humor shine through.

Bible Study & Meditation

Chapter 1: Since this week's study features a fairly long passage of Scripture, read it yourself ahead of time, so you can bring it some narrative gusto. The focus for this week is on a return to the Bible also being a return to God. In your preparation, go to God yourself. Start reading the Bible every day. Pray for breakthroughs in the lives of your group members. Pray for renewal. Pray for revived hearts, passionate to read God's word.

Chapter 2: This week, and every other week following, prioritize accountability in your group time. As a follow up from the previous week, ask your group members, "How are you doing at reading the Bible every day? What are you reading? What are you learning?" For the question time, it would be handy to gather together in advance some resources for your group to use together. Photocopy pages from some commentaries or other resources listed below. If you can't access these books, ask your pastor (who is the most likely person in your church to own some) or contact your nearest seminary to see if you can use resources from their library.

Chapter 3: Since the end goal of this week's study is to begin memorizing Scripture, print out some cards with popular Bible verses to memorize that your group members can take home. Not sure which to choose? Check out the books in the resource list below. Make sure you also leave some time this week to have group participants share their findings from their personal, in-depth Bible study project from the week before.

Chapter 4: In following up from the last study, have the group participants share the verses they worked on memorizing over the week. Encourage every effort. Don't neglect to talk about how the group is going with their regular reading of the Bible. This study's central idea is that happiness is a natural by-product of enjoying being with God in meditation. Be aware that this week's study may stir up feelings of frustration as a result of experiences of sadness or a distant God. Rather than offering answers, or passing judgments on what has been "right" or "wrong" about group members' experiences, be a good listener. Encourage them to sit and wait for God again. Pray for them.

Chapter 5: Since this study's central idea is that the Bible is God's tool that he employs to grow us, spend some time this week flipping back through the study guides and sharing what you've learned. Open your Bibles and encourage the group to share what God has revealed to them through his word. Since this is your last week together, spend some time celebrating how far you've come. Do something special. Inquire if any group member would like to continue as a Bible-reading accountability partner for someone in the group. Encourage your group members to continue their own pursuit of God's incredible word.

Additional Resources

Resources to Encourage Regular Bible Reading

- www.biblegateway.com/readingplans offers a selection of reading plans to move you through different parts of the Bible between 40 and 365 days.

- Try about.esvbible.org/resources/reading/ for other options for a daily Bible reading plan. If you do not wish to use the ESV translation, take note of the Scripture reference and read those verses in the Bible of your choice.

- Books that might inspire you to read more of the Bible include *Taking God at His Word* by Kevin DeYoung and *Eat This Book* by Eugene Peterson.

- More can be read of the Center for Bible Engagement studies at www.centerforbibleengagement.org

Resources for Studying the Bible

- *Understanding Scripture* by A. Berkeley Mickelsen and Alvera M. Mickelsen

- *Elements of Biblical Exegesis: A Basic Guide for Students and Ministers* by Michael J. Gorman

- *How to Read the Bible for All Its Worth* by Doug Stuart and Gordon Fee. It covers every type of literature found in the Bible, examining the Bible's basic building blocks. Their second volume, *How to Read the Bible Book by Book*, works through each individual book of the Bible, explaining its background and central themes.

- *An Introduction to the New Testament* by D. A. Carson and Douglas Moo

- *The New Testament: A Historical and Theological Introduction* by Donald A. Hagner

- *An Introduction to the Old Testament* by Tremper Longman III and Raymond B. Dillard

- For a list of best commentaries for each book of the Bible, visit www.bestcommentaries.com.

For Your Study of Philemon

- Peter T. O'Brien, *Colossians, Philemon*, Word Biblical Commentary

- F. F. Bruce, *The Epistles to the Colossians, to Philemon and to the Ephesians*, New International Commentary on the New Testament

- Douglas J. Moo, *The Letters to The Colossians and to Philemon*, Pillar New Testament Commentary

For Further Information on Acts

- An excellent commentary to start with is F. F. Bruce, *The Book of Acts*, New International Commentary on the New Testament.

Memorization Resources

- For those who want to follow a set plan for memorizing Bible verses, see *The Navigator's Scripture Memory Course: Topical Memory System.* This pack contains a book on how to memorize the Bible, as well as sheets of tear-off preprinted verse cards.

- For those who don't know what verses to start memorizing, see *100 Bible Verses Everyone Should Know By Heart* by Robert J. Morgan.

- For those interested in memorizing longer passages, see *An Approach to Extended Memorization of Scripture* by Andrew Davis. Reviewers have reported they were able to memorize numerous whole books of Scripture using Davis's methods.

- A great online resource is www.memverse.com.

Meditation Resources

- *Meditation and Communion with God* by John Jefferson Davis

- *Sanctuary of the Soul: Journey into Meditative Prayer* by Richard Foster

- *Savoring God's Word: Cultivating the Soul-Transforming Practice of Scripture Meditation* by Jan Johnson

- *Eat This Book* by Eugene Peterson has a section on *lectio divina*

- *The Fire of the Word: Meeting God on Holy Ground* by Chris Webb

- For further reading on the topic of *lectio divina,* see *Too Deep for Words* by Thelma Hall

EVERYDAY MATTERS BIBLE STUDIES
for women

Spiritual practices for everyday life

Acceptance	Mentoring
Bible Study & Meditation	Outreach
Celebration	Prayer
Community	Reconciliation
Confession	Sabbath Rest
Contemplation	Service
Faith	Silence
Fasting	Simplicity
Forgiveness	Solitude
Gratitude	Stewardship
Hospitality	Submission
Justice	Worship

HENDRICKSON PUBLISHERS

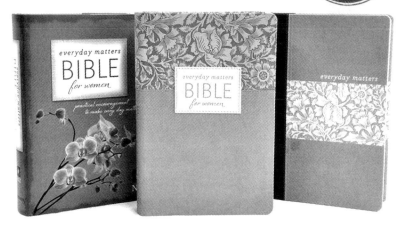